Scuba Diving

Paul Broadbent

Contents

Scuba

"Scuba" stands for **s**elf-**c**ontained **u**nderwater **b**reathing **a**pparatus. It is equipment that lets people breathe under water.

Scuba divers can stay under water for 90 minutes. These divers have been under water for 60 minutes already. How much time is left?

Some recreational divers can go down as far as 125 feet (38 m) under water.

0 ft./ 0 m

25 ft./ 7.5 m

50 ft./ 15 m

75 ft./ 23 m

100 ft./ 30 m

125 ft./ 38 m

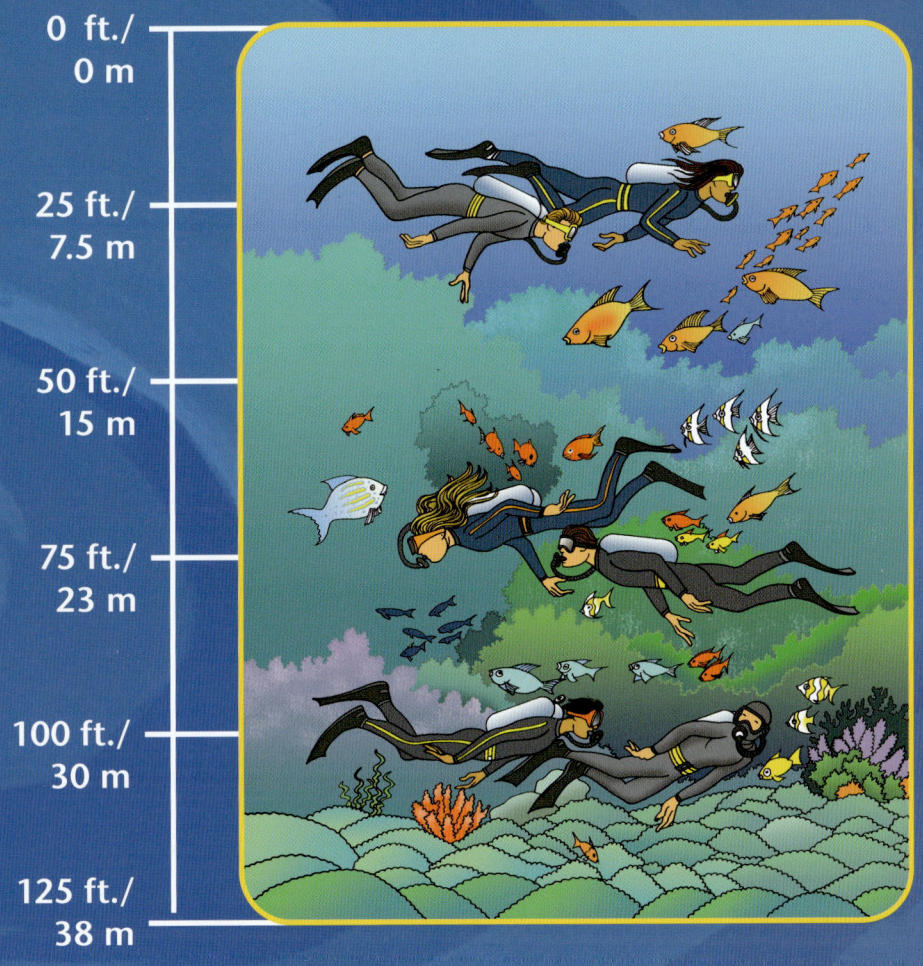

How far down have these divers gone? Use the number scale to figure it out. The top 2 divers go down another 25 feet (7.5 m). At what depth are they now?

Here, 2 of the divers are deeper than all the others. How much deeper?

TOOLS

0   10   20   30   40   50   60   70   80   90

Breathing Under Water

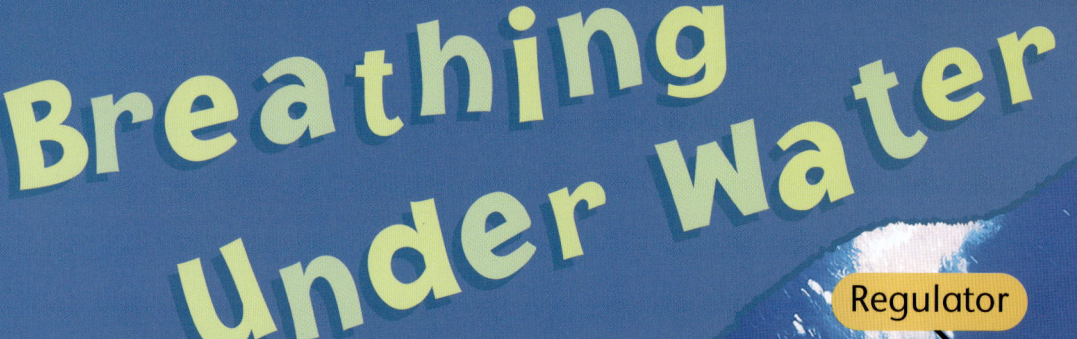

Regulator

Tank

Divers breathe slowly and deeply under water. They use a regulator to breathe in air from a tank.

The air tanks come in 4 main sizes. Look at the capacities of these tanks. Find the one that holds the most air.

8 quarts

10 quarts

12 quarts

15 quarts

What is the difference in capacity between the largest and the smallest tanks?

Many divers try their first dive in a swimming pool. It is good to practice breathing in shallow water before going deeper.

Compare the depths of these 3 divers. Which diver is at about 7.5 feet? How many feet apart are the other 2 divers?

Each diver goes up 5 feet (1.5 m). At what depth are they now?

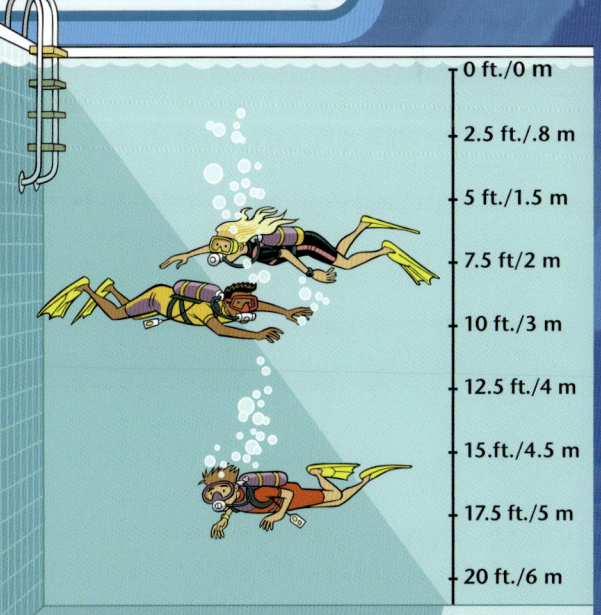

0 ft./0 m

2.5 ft./.8 m

5 ft./1.5 m

7.5 ft/2 m

10 ft./3 m

12.5 ft./4 m

15.ft./4.5 m

17.5 ft./5 m

20 ft./6 m

TOOLS

2 cups	=	1 pint
2 pints	=	1 quart
4 quarts	=	1 gallon

Going Up and Down

Divers wear a jacket that they can blow up to help them float. They let the air out of the jacket to go under water.

A depth gauge shows how deep the diver is. Divers need to make sure they don't go too deep.

A diver is 15 feet (4.5 m) down. Then she goes down another 8 feet (2.5 m). What depth is she at now? If she goes up 5 feet (1.5 m), at what depth will she be?

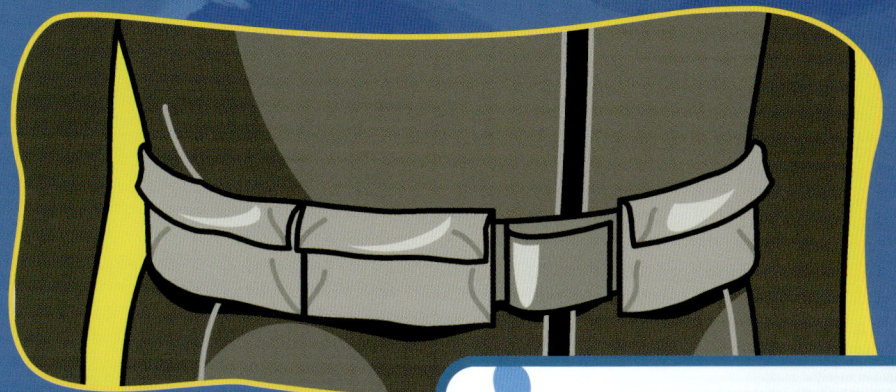

Weights are put on a belt to help a diver sink.

Here are some 1 pound (.5 kg) weights and some 2 pound (1 kg) weights.

What is the total weight of each set? How much weight is here altogether?

The diver wants to use 6 pounds (3 kg) of weight. Find different ways to make that total.

TOOLS

1	2	3	4	5	6	7	8	9	10
11	12	13	14	15	16	17	18	19	20

Dive Flags

Divers use dive flags to show where they are diving. Then boats can stay a safe distance away.

These flags can be used on a float or on a dive boat. Each flag must be at least 3.3 feet (1 m) high.

The red and white flag is 3.9 feet (1.2 m) high. The blue and white flag is 4.5 (1.4 m) feet high. Are they more or less than 3.3 feet (1 m) in height? What is the difference in their heights?

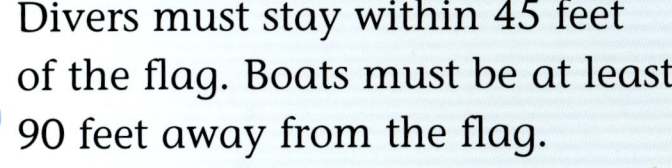

Divers must stay within 45 feet of the flag. Boats must be at least 90 feet away from the flag.

KEY WORDS

- decimals
- compare
- difference
- distance

90 ft.

75 ft.

60 ft.

45 ft.

30 ft.

15 ft.

About how far from the flag are the divers? Which divers are the closest?

How many feet is the boat from the nearest pair of divers?

TOOLS

0   15   30   45   60   75   90

Diving Equipment

Divers wear fins to help them move through the water more easily.

Here are some pairs of fins. How many fins are there altogether?

Compare the lengths of these fins. How much longer is the orange fin than the black fin? What is the difference in length between the yellow and green fins? Which fin is 15 inches shorter than the longest?

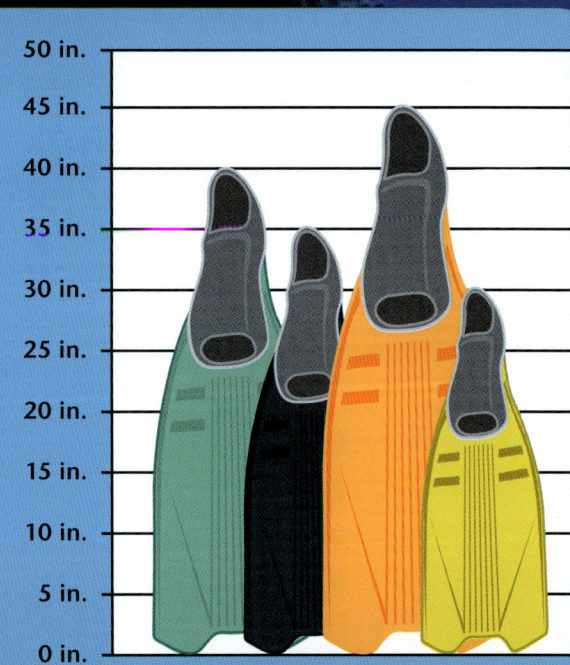

50 in.
45 in.
40 in.
35 in.
30 in.
25 in.
20 in.
15 in.
10 in.
5 in.
0 in.

KEY WORDS

- compare
- length
- shortest
- longest
- difference

Divers try not to use their arms to swim under water. Instead, they use a strong leg kick.

Divers use a snorkel when swimming at the water's surface. This way, they don't have to use air from the tank. Compare the lengths of these different snorkels. Put them in order, shortest first.

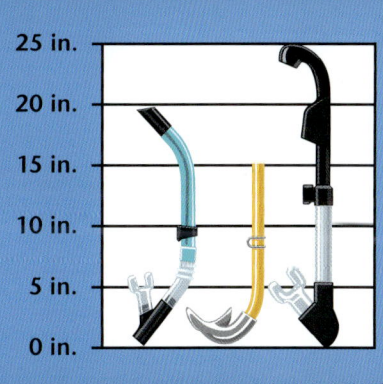

If each snorkel were 10 inches longer, what would the new lengths be?

Out on a Boat

Divers go by boat to visit different diving sites.

What time does this boat leave? What time does it arrive at the site? What time does it return?

How long is the boat at the dive site?

Diving trip

boat leaves

arrive at dive site

Dive

leave dive site

boat returns

Here are some boat journey times to different sites.

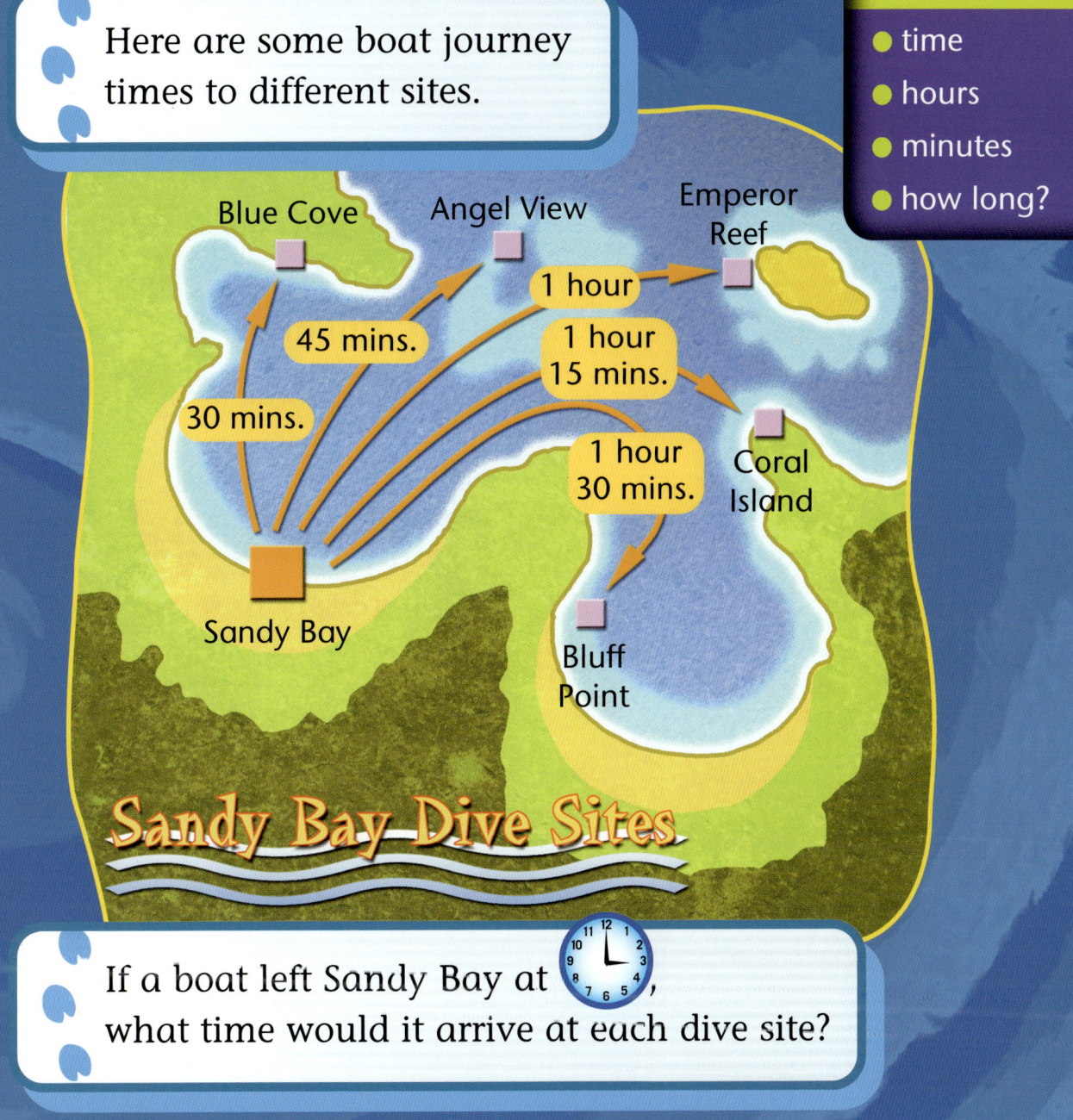

Blue Cove

Angel View

Emperor Reef

1 hour

45 mins.

1 hour 15 mins.

30 mins.

1 hour 30 mins.

Coral Island

Sandy Bay

Bluff Point

Sandy Bay Dive Sites

If a boat left Sandy Bay at [clock], what time would it arrive at each dive site?

Divers on a trip to Bluff Point dive for 1 hour and 15 minutes. If they left Sandy Bay at [clock], what time would they get back to Sandy Bay?

TOOLS

10:00 a.m. 11:00 a.m. 12:00 a.m. 1:00 p.m. 2:00 p.m. 3:00 p.m. 4:00 p.m.

5:00 p.m. 6:00 p.m. 7:00 p.m. 8:00 p.m. 9:00 p.m. 10:00 p.m. 11:00 p.m.

13

Coral Reefs

Coral reefs look like underwater gardens, full of sea life.

Coral is created by tiny animals called polyps. As they grow and die, their skeletons join together to form a coral reef.

Atoll

Coral grows in shallow water around an island.

The island sinks, leaving a ring of reefs called an atoll.

The top of the island is 125 feet (38 m) above sea level. Over a year the island sinks by 35 feet (11 m). How high above sea level is the top now?

KEY WORDS

- compare
- longest
- shortest
- estimate
- measure

Here are 6 pieces of coral.

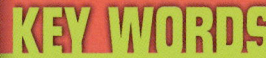

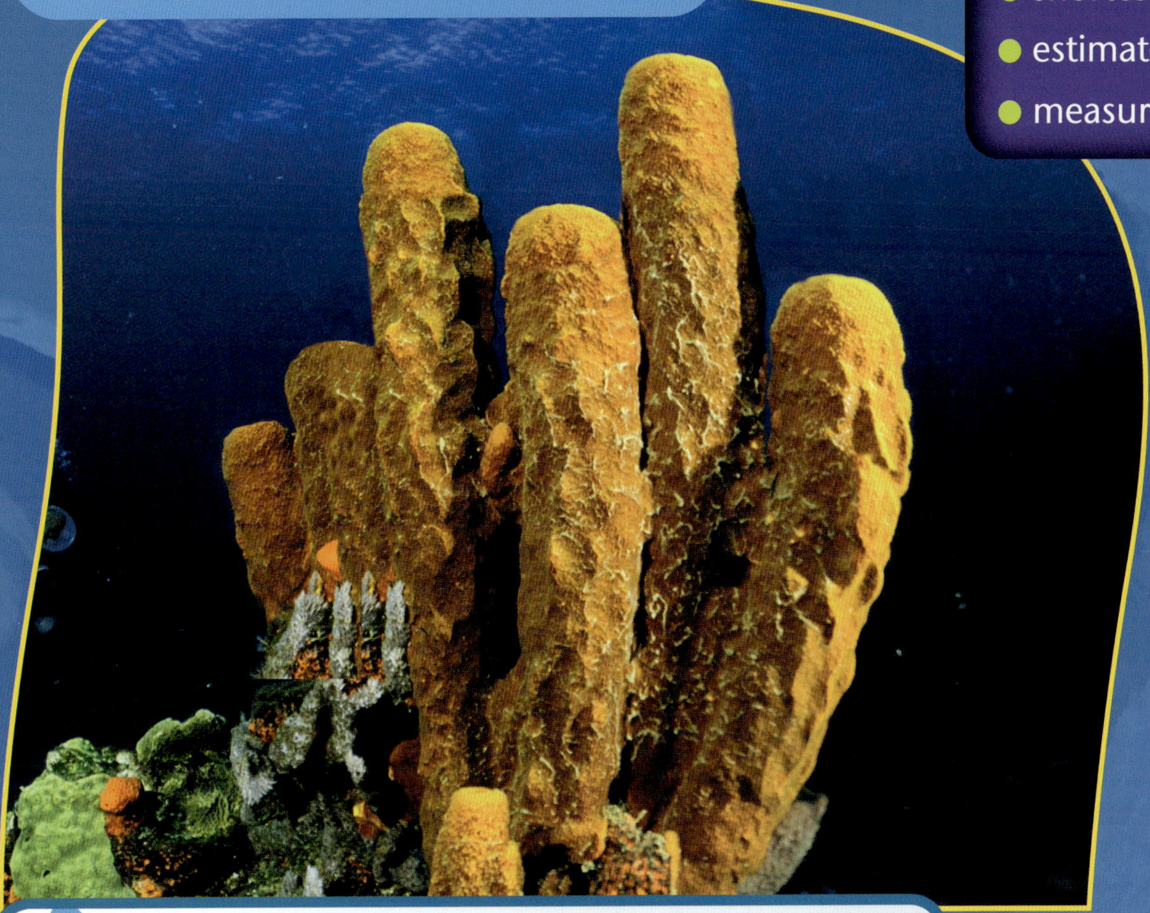

Which is the longest piece? Which is the shortest piece? Estimate their lengths and then use a ruler to measure them.

Find the difference between the longest and the shortest pieces of coral.

TOOLS

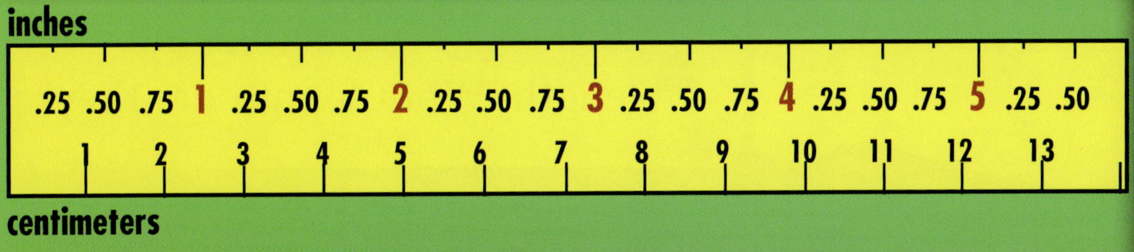
inches
.25 .50 .75 1 .25 .50 .75 2 .25 .50 .75 3 .25 .50 .75 4 .25 .50 .75 5 .25 .50
1 2 3 4 5 6 7 8 9 10 11 12 13
centimeters

Sea Turtles

Some divers go swimming with sea turtles.

Sea turtles lay their eggs in the sand. When they hatch, the baby turtles run into the sea.

inches

0   1   2   3

How long is this egg? Some turtle eggs are double this length. What length are they?

The largest kind of sea turtle is the huge leatherback sea turtle. These are the lengths of some different sea turtles.

Leatherback
sea turtle
100 in./254 cm

Hawksbill
sea turtle
40 in./100 cm

Loggerhead
sea turtle
36 in./91 cm

Green
sea turtle
30 in./76 cm

What is the difference in length between the green sea turtle and the hawksbill sea turtle? How many feet long is the loggerhead sea turtle?

True or false? The leatherback sea turtle is the same length as the other 3 sea turtles put together.

Sea turtles are fast swimmers. Some can swim at a speed of 35 miles (56 km) per hour.

TOOLS

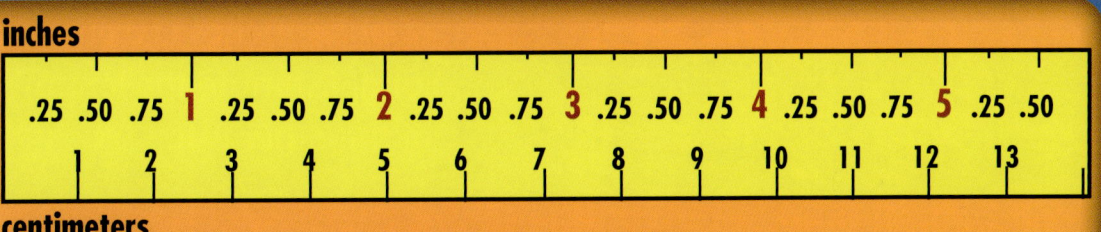

inches

.25 .50 .75 1 .25 .50 .75 2 .25 .50 .75 3 .25 .50 .75 4 .25 .50 .75 5 .25 .50

1   2   3   4   5   6   7   8   9   10   11   12   13

centimeters

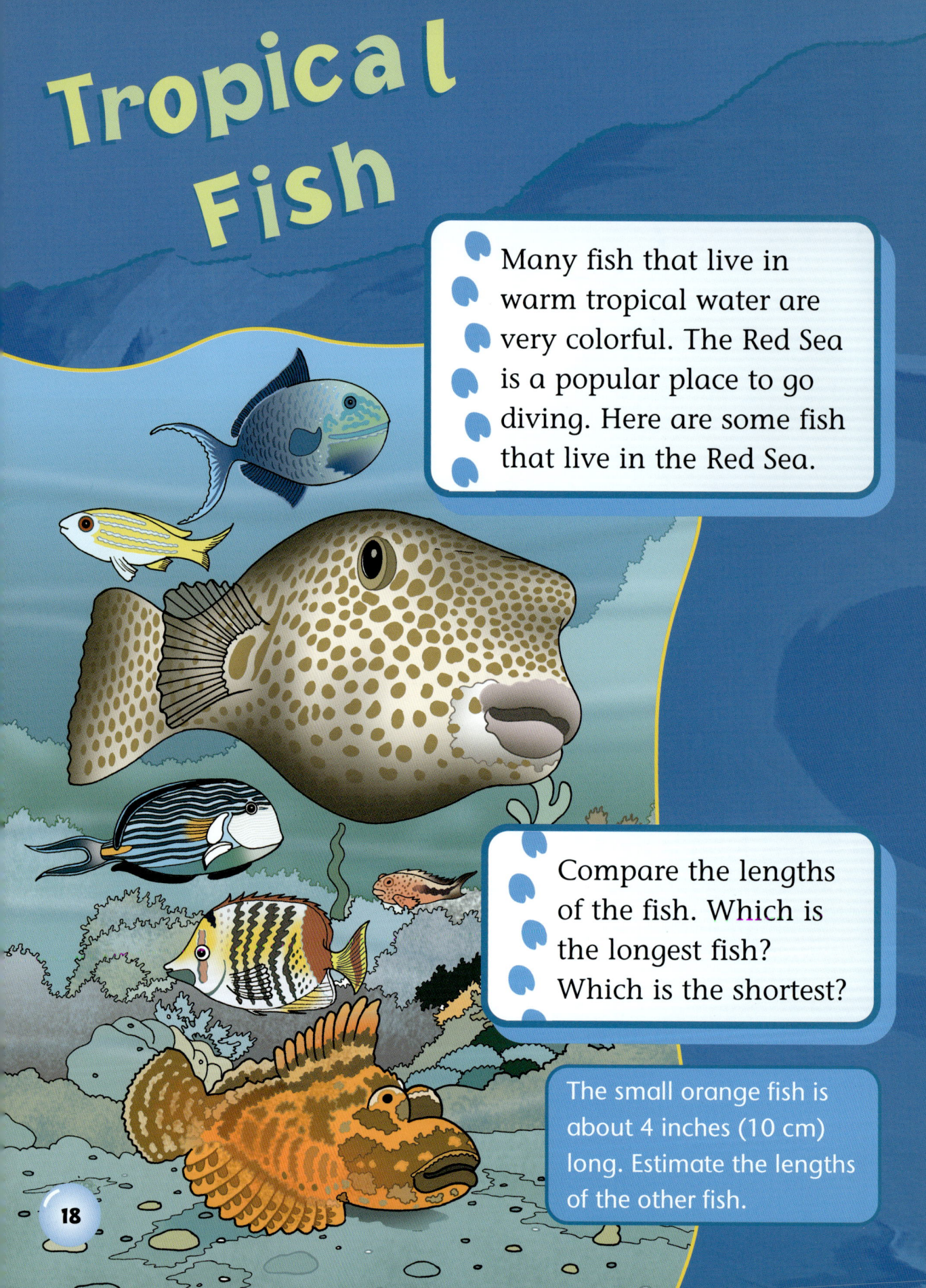

Tropical Fish

Many fish that live in warm tropical water are very colorful. The Red Sea is a popular place to go diving. Here are some fish that live in the Red Sea.

Compare the lengths of the fish. Which is the longest fish? Which is the shortest?

The small orange fish is about 4 inches (10 cm) long. Estimate the lengths of the other fish.

Here are the lengths of some fish that live in the Red Sea.

KEY WORDS

- compare
- longest
- shortest
- size
- estimate

Name	Length (in./cm)
Bigeye barracuda	30/75
Clownfish	6/15
Dartfish	4/10
Dusky batfish	18/45
False stonefish	12/30
Parrotfish	35/90
Red lionfish	16/40
Round herring	2/5
Royal angelfish	10/25
Soldierfish	24/60

Which fish is 4 inches (10 cm) longer than the clownfish?
Put the fish in order, shortest first.

The largest fish is the whale shark. It grows up to 40 feet (12 m) long and has 11 or 12 rows of teeth. Each tooth is less than 1 inch (2 mm).

Which fish is longer than the dartfish but shorter than the red lionfish?

TOOLS

0   10   20   30   40   50   60   70   80   90   100

Swimming with Dolphins

Dolphins are intelligent, friendly mammals.

Dolphins make a clicking sound. The noise bounces off nearby objects. This echo tells the dolphin if another creature is close. It warns them of danger.

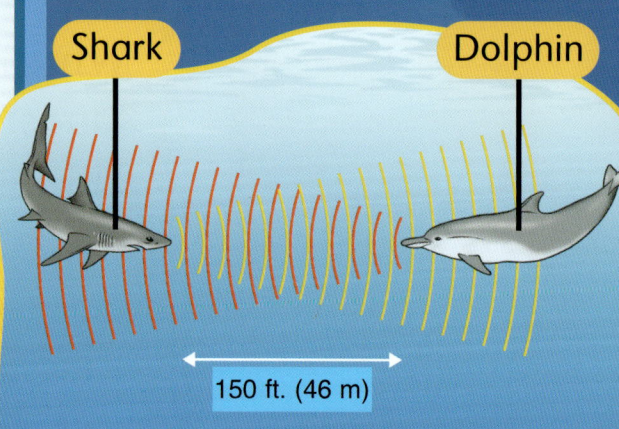

Shark

Dolphin

150 ft. (46 m)

How far apart are the shark and the dolphin? If the dolphin swims another 40 feet (12 m) away, now how far is it from the shark?

Here are some different kinds of dolphin. Compare their lengths and weights.

Common dolphin

90 in.   210 lbs.

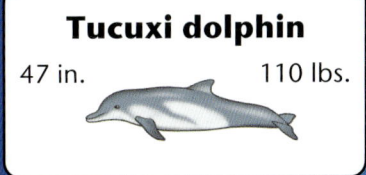

Tucuxi dolphin

47 in.   110 lbs.

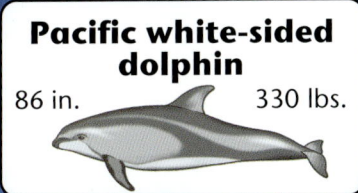

Pacific white-sided dolphin

86 in.   330 lbs.

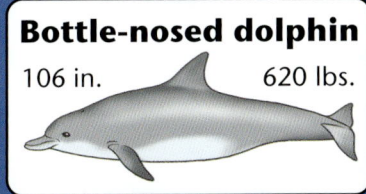

Bottle-nosed dolphin

106 in.   620 lbs.

Atlantic spotted dolphin

83 in.   220 lbs.

Which is the longest dolphin?

Which dolphins are less than 8 feet in length?

Which dolphins are heavier than the Atlantic spotted dolphin?

How much heavier is the bottle-nosed dolphin than the Atlantic spotted dolphin?

FACT!

Whales and dolphins swim by moving their tails up and down. Fish move their tails from side to side.

TOOLS

0   50   100   150   200   250   300

Shipwrecks

Skillful divers may explore shipwrecks. Some wrecks are very deep. This one is 150 feet (46 m) below the surface.

FACT!

Divers may get a sickness called "the bends" if they try to reach the surface too quickly.

When divers return to the surface, they must come up slowly – only 50 feet (15 m) each minute. How long will it take these divers to come up to the surface?

Another wreck is 100 feet (30 m) deep. Will it take more time or less time to return to the surface?

Dive	Weight of coins
1	7 ounces
2	18 ounces
3	10 ounces
4	28 ounces

This diver has found some old coins. It took 4 dives to collect all the coins. These are the weights of the coins collected on each dive.

What was the weight collected on the 3rd dive? What was the weight of coins collected altogether in the first 2 dives? How much more was collected on the last dive than the first dive?

What weight of coins was collected altogether?

TOOLS

Feet	0	25	50	75	100	125	150	175	200

Minute	0		1		2		3		4

Sum It Up

Which diver is deeper than 10 feet? What is the difference in depth between diver A and diver C?

The divers go under the water at 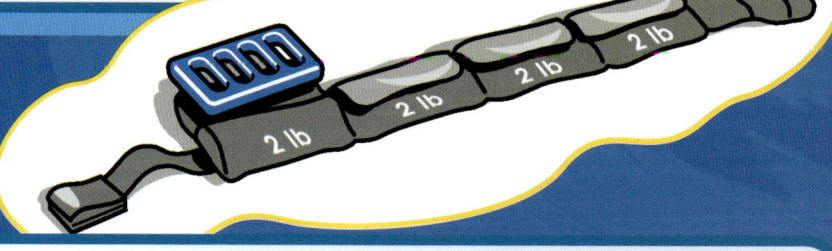. If they dive for 15 minutes, what time do they come up?

Each weight is 2 pounds (1 kg). What is the total weight on the belt?

The belt is 3 feet (.9 m) long. When it is put on, 6 inches (15 cm) of belt is hanging loose. How many inches of belt is around the waist?